Concise
Professional Services Contract 2020

Architectural Services

RIBA Concise Professional Services Contract 2020: Architectural Services

Contract Checklist

ONCE THE CONTRACT DETAILS HAVE BEEN COMPLETED, AND BEFORE THE AGREEMENT IS SIGNED, CHECK THIS LIST TO ENSURE THAT ALL OF THE KEY TERMS HAVE BEEN CONSIDERED.

YES

Has the Project Brief and Client's statement of requirements been agreed? ☐

Has the target Construction Cost been agreed/advised? ☐

Has the target Project Programme been agreed? ☐

Have any Other Client Appointments been agreed? ☐

Have the fees and expenses and payment frequency been agreed? ☐

Has the amount of professional indemnity insurance that is to be allowed for the Project been agreed and has this been arranged? ☐

Has the Architect/Consultant explained its internal complaints procedure to the Client and has a dispute resolution process been agreed in case something goes wrong? ☐

Has the Schedule of Services been completed and agreed? ☐

Has the Client been made aware that it has duties under the CDM Regulations 2015? ☐

Have all the Contract Details been completed? ☐

RIBA Concise Professional Services Contract 2020: Architectural Services

Agreement

This Agreement is between:

the Client (refer to item A of the Contract Details for full information)

AND

the Architect/Consultant (refer to item B of the Contract Details for full information)

who agree as follows:

- The Architect/Consultant shall undertake the Services set out in the Schedule of Services and shall perform the Architect/Consultant's obligations in accordance with the terms of the Contract.

- The Client shall pay the Architect/Consultant the fees and expenses set out in the Contract Details for the Services and shall perform the Client's obligations in accordance with the terms of the Contract.

- The Contract is the RIBA Concise Professional Services Contract 2020 for Architectural Services.

Signed/Executed as a: simple contract   deed

For and on behalf of the Client *(complete as appropriate)*:

Client **is not** a registered company/LLP

Name:

Signature:

Client's signature witnessed by:

Name:

Address:

Signature:

© Royal Institute of British Architects 2020

OR

Client **is** a registered company/LLP

Company registration number:

First signatory (Director/Company Secretary/Partner/Member):
Name:
Signature:

Client's signature witnessed by:
Name:
Address:

Signature:

Second signatory (Director/Company Secretary/Partner/Member) – *optional*:
Name:
Signature:

For and on behalf of the Architect/Consultant *(complete as appropriate)*:

Architect/Consultant **is not** a registered company/LLP
Name:
Signature:

Architect/Consultant's signature witnessed by:
Name:
Address:

Signature:

OR

Architect/Consultant **is** a registered company/LLP

Company registration number:

VAT registration number:

First signatory (Director/Company Secretary/Partner/Member):

Name:

Signature:

Architect/Consultant's signature witnessed by:

Name:

Address:

Signature:

Second signatory (Director/Company Secretary/Partner/Member) – *optional*:

Name:

Signature:

This Agreement is dated and delivered on:

RIBA Concise Professional Services Contract 2020: Architectural Services

Contract Details

A. The Client

Name:

Address:

Registered address (if different):

Telephone number:

Email address:

Named representative *(insert the name of a representative with authority to act on behalf of the Client for all purposes under the Contract)*:

B.   The Architect/Consultant

Name:

Address:

Registered address
(if different):

Telephone number:

Email address:

Point of contact *(insert the name of a primary point of contact with authority to act on behalf of the Architect/Consultant for all purposes under the Contract)*:

The name of the person that the Client should contact if it wishes to invoke the Architect/Consultant's internal complaints procedure:

C.   Site Address

D. Project Brief

Project description and Client's statement of requirements:

Additional briefing documents provided *(include reference numbers and dates)*:

Document	Reference number	Date

Continue on a separate sheet if necessary.

Construction Cost
The Construction Cost, as defined in the Contract Conditions, is: £

Project Programme
Key project dates, e.g. submission of planning application, commencement/completion of building works *(insert as appropriate)*:

Item	Target date

Continue on a separate sheet if necessary.

E. Other Client Appointments

Other consultant or services appointments which have been or will need to be made by the Client to enable the Architect/Consultant to undertake its work in connection with the Project are as follows:

Role:

Role:

Role:

Role:

Continue on a separate sheet if necessary.

F. Basic Fee

The basis of the Basic Fee at each stage (excluding VAT) shall be as stated below, e.g. specified percentage of Construction Cost, fixed lump sum, time charge, design cost per square metre (gross or net) or other agreed method.

Fees may be a total for each stage. The Services being undertaken are to be as stated in the Schedule of Services and the fees, excluding VAT, are as follows and are to be paid in accordance with item I of the Contract Details:

Stage	Notes	Fee

Continue on a separate sheet if necessary.

Other services:

Continue on a separate sheet if necessary.

VAT
VAT applies or does not apply to the Basic Fee *(please specify)*:

☐ VAT applies

☐ VAT does not apply

Meetings
The Architect/Consultant shall attend the following meetings during the Project:

Stage	Purpose	Total number and/or frequency allowed for	Fee[1]
Stage 0			
Stage 1			
Stage 2			
Stage 3			
Stage 4			
Stage 5			
Stage 6			

Site inspections
The Architect/Consultant shall visit the site for the purposes set out in the Schedule of Services as follows:

Stage	Total number and/or frequency allowed for	Fee[1]
Stage 5		
Stage 6		

Where additional site inspections are necessary, or requested in writing by the Client, in addition to those identified above, the Architect/Consultant shall apply time charges, as set out in item G of the Contract Details.

---

[1] State whether the fee for attending these meetings is included in the Basic Fee (insert 'BF') or will be provided on a time-based charge (insert 'TC').

G. Time Charges

Time charges for any additional fees, and/or where the Basic Fee incorporates time charges, shall be calculated on the basis of the following rates:

Person/grade	Rate, excluding VAT *(state whether £ per hour or £ per day)*

Continue on a separate sheet if necessary.

H. Expenses

The specified expenses are as follows:

Continue on a separate sheet if necessary.

The specified expenses listed above, excluding VAT, shall be charged:

- at net cost plus a handling charge, which shall be calculated at the following percentage of net cost   %

- by the addition of the following fee to the total fee £

- by the addition of   % to the Basic Fee

- other *(please specify)*

Other expenses, including disbursements, such as payments to the local authority for planning and Building Regulations submissions, shall be charged at net cost plus the following percentage of net cost   %

Where applicable, travel shall be charged at the following rate per mile £

Hard copies of drawings and documents shall be charged at the following rate per page:

	A4	A3	A2	A1	A0
Black and white	£	£	£	£	£
Full colour	£	£	£	£	£

I. Payment

Payment Notices for instalments of fees, time charges and expenses shall be issued and paid:

- [ ] on a weekly basis
- [ ] on a monthly basis
- [ ] at the end of each stage
- [ ] in accordance with the agreed drawdown schedule dated _____ ref: _____
- [ ] other *(please specify)*

J. Professional Indemnity Insurance

The amount of professional indemnity insurance cover to be maintained for the Project in respect of each and every claim or series of claims arising out of the same originating cause shall be £ _____

Professional indemnity insurance cover shall be maintained by the Architect/Consultant for the above amount, except for claims arising out of:

- [ ] pollution or contamination, with an aggregate limit of £ _____
    - [ ] annually OR [ ] per project

- [ ] asbestos, with an aggregate limit of £ _____
    - [ ] annually OR [ ] per project

- [ ] cladding or fire-related issues,[2] with an aggregate limit of £ _____
    - [ ] annually OR [ ] per project

- [ ] other[2,3] *(please specify)*

    _____

    with an aggregate limit of £ _____
    - [ ] annually OR [ ] per project

---

[2] It is important to ensure that this wording reflects the wording of any restrictions in the Architect/Consultant's professional indemnity insurance policy.

[3] Specify other material exclusions or restrictions under the Architect/Consultant's professional indemnity insurance that are relevant to the Project.

K. Dispute Resolution

Mediation
The Parties may agree to try to resolve their differences through mediation without prejudice to any other dispute resolution rights.

Adjudication
Either Party has the statutory right (but no obligation) to refer a dispute, at any time, to adjudication. If a dispute is so referred, the Scheme for Construction Contracts (England and Wales) Regulations 1998 as amended shall apply. The Adjudicator's decision is binding unless and until the dispute is determined by arbitration or litigation following referral by either Party.

Final Dispute Resolution Process
The Parties may select either arbitration or litigation. If the Parties do not make a selection then litigation shall be the final dispute resolution process.

Arbitration ☐ Applies
The Parties select arbitration for final dispute resolution.

OR

Litigation ☐ Applies
The Parties select court proceedings for final dispute resolution.

If the Parties cannot reach agreement on a person to act as Mediator, Adjudicator or Arbitrator, either Party may apply for a nomination or appointment to be made by the Royal Institute of British Architects.

L. Information Formats

Drawings and documents produced by the Architect/Consultant using computer aided design (CAD), any other proprietary software or building information modelling (BIM) in connection with the Services shall be provided in the following format:

☐ Drawings and documents produced by the Architect/Consultant shall be provided to the Client in PDF format only.

OR

☐ Information, drawings and documents produced by the Architect/Consultant shall be provided to the Client in PDF format and in the file format(s) listed below on the condition that the PDF format files take precedence and the Architect/Consultant is not liable for any loss or degradation of information resulting from the translation from the original file format to any other file format or from the recipient's reading of it in any other software or another version of the software referred to below:

Software (e.g. AutoCAD, Revit, ArchiCAD)	Version	File format (e.g. dwg, dxf, dgn, ifc, rvt)	Type of data (e.g. 2D or 3D CAD files, BIM models, spreadsheets, etc.)

OR

☐ Information produced by the Architect/Consultant shall be provided to the Client in accordance with the agreed BIM protocol dated _____ ref: _____

Contract Conditions

Definition of Terms

Architect[4]/Consultant: the person or organisation that the Client appoints to perform the Services.

Basic Fee: the fee for the Services excluding VAT and any additional charges, such as expenses, disbursements, etc.

Building Contract: the contract between the Client and the Contractor for the construction of the Project.

CDM Regulations 2015: the Construction (Design and Management) Regulations 2015 and any guidance as issued, amended or replaced from time to time by the Health and Safety Executive, which govern the management of health, safety and welfare for construction projects.

Client: the person or organisation referred to in item A of the Contract Details. This also includes the Client's representative where one is appointed by the Client with full authority to act on behalf of the Client for all purposes in connection with the matters set out in the Contract, except where advised to the contrary.

Confidential Information: all information relating to the Project and the Client's and Architect/Consultant's business and affairs which either Party directly or indirectly receives or acquires from the other Party or any representative of the other Party whether in writing, by electronic mail or orally and which is not otherwise already in the public domain.

Construction Cost: the Client's target cost for the building works as specified in the Project Brief, as set out in item D of the Contract Details (being the Client's initial budget), and subsequently the latest estimate approved by the Client or, where applicable, the actual cost of constructing the Project upon agreement or determination of the final account for the Project. The Construction Cost includes the cost of any equipment and/or materials provided or to be provided by the Client to the Contractor for installation as part of the Project, and any direct works carried out by or on behalf of the Client. The Construction Cost excludes VAT, professional fees, the cost of resolution of any dispute, the Client's legal and in-house expenses and any loss and/or expense payments made to the Contractor and is not affected by any liquidated damages deducted by the Client.

Contractor: the party referred to as the Contractor in the Building Contract.

Final Date for Payment: the date, specified in clause 5.13, by which a payment that is due shall be paid.

Health and Safety File: the file required by the CDM Regulations 2015, which contains relevant health and safety information needed to allow future construction works, including cleaning, maintenance, alterations, refurbishment and demolition, to be carried out safely.

Notified Sum: the sum set out in a Payment Notice or in a default notice.

---

[4] 'Architect' is a legally protected title in the UK, which can only be used by people registered under the Architects Act 1997 with the Architects Registration Board (ARB).

Other Client Appointments: other consultant or services appointments which have been, or will need to be, made by the Client to enable the Architect/Consultant to undertake its work in connection with the Project.

Party/Parties: the signatories to the Agreement: the Client and the Architect/Consultant described in items A and B of the Contract Details.

Payment Notice: a notice that the Architect/Consultant issues to the Client, in accordance with clauses 5.10 to 5.15, showing the payment that the Architect/Consultant considers is due and how it was calculated.

Practical Completion: when the works are certified as having achieved 'Practical Completion' under the terms of the Building Contract.

Principal Contractor: a contractor appointed by the Client as Principal Contractor under the CDM Regulations 2015.

Principal Designer: a designer appointed by the Client as Principal Designer under the CDM Regulations 2015.

Project: as described in the Project Brief, item D of the Contract Details.

Project Brief: the Client's requirements for the Project, as initially set out in item D of the Contract Details and including any revisions made by the Architect/Consultant and approved by the Client.

Project Programme: the Client's initial programme for the Project, as specified in item D of the Contract Details, and including any revisions made by the Architect/Consultant and approved by the Client.

Schedule of Services: the schedule specifying the Services and additional services to be undertaken by the Architect/Consultant in connection with the Project, which is incorporated into the Contract.

Services: the professional services to be performed by the Architect/Consultant specified in the Schedule of Services, which may be varied by agreement.

Clauses

1. General Interpretation

1.1 Where under the Contract an action is required to be taken within a specified period, in calculating a period, a day shall be a calendar day and a date shall be a calendar date. When a period is calculated it shall exclude public holidays.

1.2 The provisions of the Contract continue to bind the Client and the Architect/Consultant as long as is necessary to give effect to the Parties' respective rights and obligations.

1.3 The Contract supersedes any previous agreement or arrangements between the Client and the Architect/Consultant in relation to the Services (whether oral or written) and represents the entire agreement between the Client and the Architect/Consultant in relation to the Services. All additions, amendments and variations to the Contract shall be binding only if agreed in writing by duly authorised representatives of both the Client and the Architect/Consultant.

1.4 If any clause or part of any clause of the Contract is ruled by the courts or declared to be invalid or unenforceable in any way, it shall be severed from the Contract and this shall not affect any other clause of the Contract, nor the validity of the remaining clauses of the Contract, which shall remain in full force.

1.5 The Contract is subject to the law of England and Wales and the Parties submit to the exclusive jurisdiction of the courts of England and Wales.

1.6 Subject to clause 3.1 of the Contract Conditions, to the extent that either Party processes personal data, as part of the Contract, the Party undertakes to do so in compliance with the General Data Protection Regulation (GDPR) and to keep such personal data in a secure technological environment.

2. Client's Responsibilities

2.1 The Client shall:

    2.1.1 inform the Architect/Consultant of the Project Brief, the Construction Cost, the Project Programme and the Services required and, as soon as reasonably practicable, of any subsequent changes required and agree steps to mitigate the consequences of such changes

    2.1.2 provide, free of charge, information in the Client's possession, or which is reasonably obtainable, and which the Architect/Consultant reasonably advises is necessary for the proper and timely performance of the Services, and the Architect/Consultant shall be entitled to rely on such information

    2.1.3 make decisions and give approvals as necessary for the proper and timely performance of the Services

    2.1.4 appoint or otherwise engage any Other Client Appointments required to perform work or services under separate agreements and require them to collaborate with the Architect/Consultant. The Client shall confirm in writing to the Architect/Consultant the work or services to be performed by any Other Client Appointments

    2.1.5 hold the Other Client Appointments, and not the Architect/Consultant, responsible for the proper carrying out and completion of the work or services entrusted to them under any Other Client Appointments

- 2.1.6 hold the Contractor(s) appointed to undertake construction works, and not the Architect/Consultant, responsible for the proper carrying out and completion of construction works in compliance with the Building Contract
- 2.1.7 where the Architect/Consultant is appointed as Contract Administrator for the Building Contract, not deal with the Contractor directly or interfere with the Architect/Consultant's duties under the Building Contract
- 2.1.8 not hold the Architect/Consultant responsible for any instructions issued by the Client to the Other Client Appointments or Contractor
- 2.1.9 pay any statutory charges and any fees, expenses and disbursements in respect of any obligations for planning, building control and other consents.

2.2 The Client may issue reasonable instructions to the Architect/Consultant. The Client's named representative, as indicated in item A of the Contract Details, shall have full authority to act on behalf of the Client for all purposes in connection with the matters set out in the Contract.

2.3 The Client acknowledges that the Architect/Consultant does not warrant:
- 2.3.1 that planning permission and other approvals from third parties shall be granted at all or, if granted, will be granted in accordance with any anticipated timescale
- 2.3.2 compliance with any Project Programme and Construction Cost, which may need to be reviewed for, but not limited to:
  - (a) variations instructed by the Client
  - (b) fluctuations in market prices
  - (c) delays caused by any Other Client Appointments, the Contractor or any other factor that is not the responsibility of the Architect/Consultant under the Contract
  - (d) the discovery at any time of previously unknown factors which were not reasonably foreseeable at the date of the Contract
- 2.3.3 the competence, performance, work, services, products or solvency of any Other Client Appointments or the Contractor.

2.4 The Client shall not disclose Confidential Information unless:
- 2.4.1 disclosure is necessary to take professional advice in relation to the Contract or the Services
- 2.4.2 it is already in the public domain other than due to wrongful use or disclosure by the Client
- 2.4.3 disclosure is required by law or because of disputes arising out of or in connection with the Contract.

3. Architect/Consultant's Responsibilities

3.1 In the performance of the Services, and discharging all the obligations under the Contract, the Architect/Consultant will exercise the reasonable skill, care and diligence to be expected of an Architect/Consultant experienced in the provision of such services for projects of a similar size, nature and complexity to the Project. Notwithstanding anything that may appear elsewhere to the contrary, whether under this Contract or otherwise, the Architect/Consultant's duties and obligations shall be deemed to be subject to the exercise of such reasonable skill, care and diligence and nothing contained in this Agreement or elsewhere shall be construed as imposing on the Architect/Consultant any greater duty than the exercise of such reasonable skill, care and diligence.

3.2 The Architect/Consultant shall:
- 3.2.1 perform the Services with due regard to the Project Brief

3.2.2 inform the Client of progress in the performance of the Services and, upon becoming aware, of any issue that may materially affect the Project Brief, Project Programme, Construction Cost or quality of the Project, and any information, decision or action required in mitigation

3.2.3 inform the Client of a need to make any Other Client Appointments to perform work in connection with the Project and/or any information, decision or action required from the Client or Other Client Appointments in connection with the performance of the Services

3.2.4 act on behalf of the Client in the matters set out in the Contract or in relation to any project procedures agreed with the Client from time to time, subject to the Client's prior written approval

3.2.5 if acting as Contract Administrator for the Building Contract, exercise impartial and independent judgement when acting as an intermediary between the Client and the Contractor

3.2.6 collaborate with any Other Client Appointments named in the Contract Details or any other parties who might reasonably be expected to perform work or services and, where indicated in the Services, the Architect/Consultant shall coordinate relevant information received from such persons with the Architect/Consultant's design, but the Architect/Consultant shall not be responsible for the content of the information received

3.2.7 make no material alteration to the Services or an approved design without the prior written consent of the Client, except in an emergency, whereupon the Architect/Consultant shall confirm such actions to the Client without delay.

3.3 Subject to clause 3.4, the Architect/Consultant shall have the right to publish photographs and other information relating to the Project, and the Client shall give reasonable access to the Project for this purpose for 2 years after Practical Completion.

3.4 The Architect/Consultant shall not disclose Confidential Information unless:

3.4.1 disclosure is necessary for the proper performance of the Services, or in order to take professional advice in relation to the Contract or the Services, or in order to obtain/maintain insurance cover as required by the Contract

3.4.2 it is already in the public domain other than due to wrongful use or disclosure by the Architect/Consultant

3.4.3 disclosure is required by law or because of disputes arising out of or in connection with the Contract.

4. Assignment, Subcontracting, Novation and Third Party Rights

4.1 Neither the Architect/Consultant nor the Client shall at any time assign the benefit of the Contract or any rights arising under it without the prior written consent of the other. Such consent shall not be unreasonably withheld or delayed.

4.2 The Architect/Consultant shall not subcontract performance of any part of the Services without the prior consent of the Client, and such consent shall not be unreasonably withheld or delayed. Any such subcontracting shall not relieve the Architect/Consultant of responsibility for carrying out and completing the Services in accordance with the Contract. Such consent shall not be required for agency or self-employed staff.

4.3 The Parties may, by agreement, novate the Contract on terms to be agreed.

4.4 There is no intention to grant rights to third parties pursuant to the Contracts (Rights of Third Parties) Act 1999, other than to lawful assignees.

5. Fees and Expenses

5.1 The fees for performance of the Services and/or any additional services shall be calculated in accordance with this clause and as specified in the Contract Details.

5.2 The Basic Fee for performance of the Services shall be as specified in item F of the Contract Details and may be any or a combination of:

5.2.1 the specified percentage or percentages applied to the Construction Cost. Until the actual cost of the building work is known, the percentages are applied to the latest approved estimate of the cost of the building work or the Building Contract sum. The total fee shall be adjusted based on the final Construction Cost on completion of the Services. The cost shall exclude VAT, fees and any claims made by or against the Contractor

5.2.2 the separate percentages specified for each RIBA Plan of Work stage applied to the Construction Cost at the end of the previous stage

5.2.3 the specified lump sum or sums

5.2.4 the time charges ascertained by multiplying the time reasonably spent in the performance of the Services by the specified hourly or daily rate for the relevant personnel, as set out in item G of the Contract Details. Time 'reasonably spent' includes the time spent in connection with performance of the Services in travelling from and returning to the Architect/Consultant's office

5.2.5 any other agreed method.

5.3 Lump sums and rates for time charges, mileage and printing shall be revised every 12 months in accordance with changes in the Consumer Prices Index. Each 12-month period commences on the anniversary of the date of the Contract.

5.4 The Basic Fee shall be adjusted:

5.4.1 including due allowance for any loss and/or expense, if material changes are made to the Project Brief and/or the latest approved estimate of the cost of the building work and/or Project Programme save to the extent that any changes arise from a breach of the Contract by the Architect/Consultant and/or the Services are varied by agreement

5.4.2 where percentage fees in accordance with clause 5.2.1 or 5.2.2 apply, to compensate the Architect/Consultant for any reduction of the Construction Cost arising solely from deflationary market conditions not prevailing at the date of the Contract

5.4.3 if the Client instructs a reduction in the Project Brief during the performance of the Services, or there is a reduction in the Construction Cost due to deflationary market conditions, the figure to which the percentage Basic Fee shall be applied, up to the date of the instruction or reduction, shall be the current professionally prepared estimate of the Construction Cost or the lowest acceptable tender (whichever is later) immediately prior to the instruction or reduction.

5.5 Subject to clause 5.6, if the Architect/Consultant is involved in extra work or incurs extra expense for reasons beyond the Architect/Consultant's reasonable control, additional fees shall be calculated on a time basis in accordance with clause 5.2.4 at the rate(s) set out in item G of the Contract Details unless otherwise agreed. Matters in relation to which the Architect/Consultant shall be entitled to additional fees include, but are not limited to, where:

5.5.1 the cost of any work, installation or equipment, in connection with which the Architect/Consultant performs Services, is not included in the Construction Cost

5.5.2 the Architect/Consultant is required to vary any Service already commenced or completed or to provide a new design after the Client has authorised development of an approved design

	5.5.3	the nature of the Project reasonably requires that substantial parts of the design are not completed or that they are specified provisionally or approximately before construction commences
	5.5.4	performance of the Services is delayed, disrupted or prolonged.
5.6		The Architect/Consultant shall inform the Client on becoming aware that clause 5.5 shall apply. Clause 5.5 shall not apply to the extent that any change or extra work or expense arises from a breach of the Contract by the Architect/Consultant.
5.7		The Client shall reimburse the Architect/Consultant for expenses and disbursements in the manner specified in item H of the Contract Details.
5.8		The Architect/Consultant shall maintain records of time spent on Services performed on a time basis and for any expenses and disbursements to be reimbursed at net cost. The Architect/Consultant shall make such records available to the Client on reasonable request.
5.9		Where the Architect/Consultant is instructed by the Client to invite a tender or tenders for work or services in connection with the Project but no tender is submitted or accepted, the Architect/Consultant shall be entitled to fees due up to and including the receipt of tenders based on the construction work or that part of it relating to the Services current at the date of tender.

Payment Notices

5.10		The Architect/Consultant shall issue Payment Notices at the intervals specified in item I of the Contract Details.
5.11		In the event of non-payment of any amount properly due to the Architect/Consultant under the Contract, the Architect/Consultant is entitled to interest on the unpaid amounts under the provisions of clause 5.22. The Architect/Consultant may:
	5.11.1	suspend use of the copyright licence under the provisions of clause 6
	5.11.2	suspend or terminate performance of the Services and other obligations under the provisions of clause 9
	5.11.3	commence dispute resolution procedures and/or debt recovery procedures.
5.12		Each Payment Notice shall comprise the Architect/Consultant's account, setting out any accrued instalments of the fee and other amounts due, less any amounts previously paid, and stating the basis of calculation of the amount specified, which shall be the Notified Sum. The payment due date shall be the date of the Architect/Consultant's Payment Notice. Instalments of fees shall be calculated on the Architect/Consultant's reasonable estimate of the percentage of completion of the Services or stages or other services or any other specified method.
5.13		The Client shall pay the Notified Sum within 14 days of the date of issue of the relevant Payment Notice (which shall be the Final Date for Payment) unless:
	5.13.1	the Architect/Consultant has become insolvent (as defined in the Housing Grants, Construction and Regeneration Act 1996) at any time between the last date on which the Client could have issued the notice under clause 5.16 and the Final Date for Payment
	5.13.2	the Client has issued a notice under clause 5.16.
5.14		The Client shall not delay payment of any undisputed part of the Notified Sum.
5.15		The Architect/Consultant shall submit the final Payment Notice for fees and any other amounts due when the Architect/Consultant reasonably considers the Services have been completed.

Notice of Intention to Pay Less

5.16 If the Client intends to pay less than the Notified Sum, the Client shall give a written notice to the Architect/Consultant not later than 5 days before the Final Date for Payment, specifying:

    5.16.1 the amount that the Client considers to be due on the date the notice is served

    5.16.2 the basis on which that sum is calculated

    5.16.3 the ground for doing so or, if there is more than one ground, each ground and the amount attributable to it.

5.17 The Client shall, on or before the Final Date for Payment, make payment to the Architect/Consultant of the amount, if any, specified in the written notice.

5.18 If no such notice is given, the amount due and payable shall be the Notified Sum stated as due in the Architect/Consultant's account. The Client shall not delay payment of any undisputed part of the account.

5.19 If the Client issues such a notice and the matter is referred to an Adjudicator who decides that an additional sum, greater than the amount stated in the notice of intention to pay less, is due, the Client shall pay that sum within 7 days of the date of the decision or the date which, in the absence of the notice, would have been the Final Date for Payment, whichever is the later.

5.20 The Client shall not withhold any amount due to the Architect/Consultant under the Contract unless the amount has been agreed with the Architect/Consultant or has been decided by any tribunal to which the matter is referred as not being due to the Architect/Consultant. All rights of set-off at common law or in equity which the Client would otherwise be entitled to exercise are expressly excluded.

5.21 If the performance of any or all of the Services and/or obligations is suspended or terminated, the Architect/Consultant shall be entitled to:

    5.21.1 payment of any part of the fee and other amounts properly due to the date of the last instalment and a fair and reasonable amount up to the date of suspension or termination to reflect any work undertaken but not completed at the time of suspension or termination and payment of any licence fee due under clause 6

    5.21.2 reimbursement of any loss and/or damages caused to the Architect/Consultant due to the suspension or the termination, except where the Architect/Consultant is in material or persistent breach of the obligations under the Contract.

5.22 In the event that any amounts are not paid when properly due, the Architect/Consultant shall be entitled to simple interest on such amounts until the date that payment is received at 8% per year over the dealing rate of the Bank of England, current at the date that payment becomes overdue, together with such costs as are reasonably incurred by the Architect/Consultant (including costs of time spent by principals, employees and advisers) in obtaining payment of any sums due under the Contract. Any entitlement to interest at the specified rate shall also apply to any amounts that are awarded in adjudication, arbitration or legal proceedings.

5.23 The Client or the Architect/Consultant shall pay to the other Party who successfully pursues, resists or defends any claim or part of a claim brought by the other:

    5.23.1 such costs as are reasonably incurred (including costs of time spent by principals, employees and advisers) where the matter is resolved by negotiation or mediation

    5.23.2 such costs as may be determined by any dispute resolution body to which the matter is referred.

5.24 In addition to the fees and expenses, the Client shall pay any VAT chargeable on the Architect/Consultant's fees and expenses.

6. Copyright and Licence

6.1 Subject to clause 6.3, the Architect/Consultant shall own all intellectual property rights, including the copyright in the drawings and documents produced in performing the Services, and this clause generally asserts the Architect/Consultant's moral right to be identified as the author of such work.

6.2 No part of any design by the Architect/Consultant may be registered under the Registered Designs Regulations 2001 by the Client without the written consent of the Architect/Consultant.

6.3 To the extent that fees and other amounts properly due are paid, the Client shall have a licence to copy and use all drawings and documents provided by the Architect/Consultant in either paper or digital formats only for purposes related to construction of the Project or its subsequent use or sale. They may not be used for reproduction of the design for any part of any extension of the Project or any other project.

6.4 Copying or use of the drawings and documents which have been provided in either paper or digital formats by any Other Client Appointments providing services to the Project shall be deemed to be permitted under a sub-licence granted by the Client, whether such drawings and documents were issued by the Client or on the Client's behalf.

6.5 The Architect/Consultant shall be liable to the Client in respect of any reasonably foreseeable and fully mitigated expenses, losses or damages directly suffered by the Client as a result of the work of the Architect/Consultant being in breach of copyright or any other intellectual rights of any third party.

6.6 The Architect/Consultant shall not be liable for any use of the drawings and documents which have been provided in either paper or digital formats other than for the purpose for which they were prepared and provided by the Architect/Consultant.

6.7 If at any time the Client is in default of payment of any fees or other amounts properly due, the Architect/Consultant may suspend further use of the licence and any sub-licences for the drawings and documents to which the unpaid monies relate on giving 7 days' notice of the intention to do so. Use of the licence may be resumed on receipt of such outstanding amounts.

6.8 The licence shall stay in force, notwithstanding the expiry or termination of the Contract, unless it is suspended at the date of such expiry or termination.

6.9 The Basic Fee for the performance of the Services shall include all royalties, licence fees or similar expenses for the making, use or exercise by the Architect/Consultant of any invention or design patents, etc. for the purpose of performing the Services.

7. Architect/Consultant's Liability

7.1 Actions or proceedings arising out of or in connection with the Contract, whether in contract, in tort, for negligence or breach of statutory duty or otherwise, shall not be commenced after the expiry of 6 or 12 years, depending on how the Contract is executed, from the date of Practical Completion or the date of completion of the last Services, whichever is the earlier.

7.2 In any such action or proceedings:

  7.2.1 the Architect/Consultant's liability for loss or damage shall not exceed the amount of the Architect/Consultant's professional indemnity insurance specified in item J of the Contract Details

  7.2.2 no employee of the Architect/Consultant or any agent of the Architect/Consultant shall be personally liable to the Client for any negligence, default or any other liability whatsoever arising from performance of the Services.

7.3 In respect of any claim by the Client under the Contract, and without prejudice to the provisions of clause 7.2.1, the Architect/Consultant's liability shall be limited to such sum as shall be agreed between the Parties or adjudged by the court to be the proportion of the loss to the Client caused by the Architect/Consultant's failure to exercise reasonable skill, care and diligence in the performance of its duties under the Contract. This proportion is to be calculated on the basis that:

7.3.1 all other consultants, contractors and Other Client Appointments providing work or services for the Project are deemed to have provided to the Client contractual undertakings in respect of their work or services on terms materially no less onerous than those which apply to the Architect/Consultant under the Contract

7.3.2 there are deemed to be no exclusions or limitations of liability or joint insurance or co-insurance provisions between the Client and any other persons referred to in this clause

7.3.3 all the persons referred to in this clause are deemed to have paid to the Client such sums as it would be just and equitable for them to pay, having regard to the extent of their responsibility for that loss and/or damage.

8. Professional Indemnity Insurance

8.1 The Architect/Consultant shall maintain, until the expiry of the period specified in clause 7.1, professional indemnity insurance with a limit of indemnity not less than the amount or amounts specified in item J of the Contract Details, provided such insurance continues to be offered on commercially reasonable terms to the Architect/Consultant at the time when the insurance is taken out or renewed. The Architect/Consultant, when reasonably requested by the Client, shall produce for inspection a broker's letter or certificate confirming that such insurance has been obtained and is being maintained.

8.2 The Architect/Consultant shall inform the Client as soon as practicable upon becoming aware that such insurance ceases to be available on commercially reasonable terms or, subsequent to the date of the Contract, any restrictions are attached to the policy or an aggregate limit applies to any matters other than those specified in the Contract Details in order that the Architect/Consultant and the Client can discuss the best means of protecting their respective positions.

9. Suspension or Termination

9.1 The Client may suspend or terminate performance of any or all of the Services and other obligations under the Contract by giving the Architect/Consultant at least 7 days' written notice and stating the reason for doing so.

9.2 The Architect/Consultant may suspend or terminate performance of any or all of the Services and other obligations under the Contract by giving the Client at least 7 days' written notice and stating the grounds on which it intends to do so. Such grounds are limited to:

9.2.1 the Client's failure to pay any fees or other amounts due by the Final Date for Payment unless, where applicable, the Client has given effective notice under clause 5.16 of the intention to pay less than the amount stated in the Architect/Consultant's Payment Notice

9.2.2 the Client is in material or persistent breach of its obligations under the Contract

9.2.3 the Architect/Consultant is prevented from or impeded in performing the Services for reasons beyond the Architect/Consultant's control

9.2.4 force majeure

9.2.5 any other reasonable grounds for suspension or termination of the Contract.

9.3 In the event of suspension or termination, the Architect/Consultant shall cease performance of the Services and/or other obligations under the Contract in an orderly and economical manner on the expiry of the notice period after receipt or issue of a notice of suspension or termination.

9.4 If the reason for a notice of suspension arises from a default:

9.4.1 which is remedied within the notice period, the Architect/Consultant shall resume performance of the Services and other obligations under the Contract within a reasonable period

9.4.2 which is not remedied within the notice period by the defaulting Party, the Contract may be terminated by the non-defaulting Party giving at least 7 days' further written notice.

9.5 Where Services are suspended by either Party after serving notice under clause 9.1 or clause 9.2 and not resumed within 6 months, the Architect/Consultant has the right to treat performance of the Services as ended on giving at least 7 days' further written notice to the Client.

9.6 The direct or indirect effect of any period of suspension arising from a valid notice given under clause 9.1 or clause 9.2 shall be taken into account for the purposes of assessing compliance by the Architect/Consultant with the Project Programme.

9.7 Performance of the Services and/or other obligations may be terminated immediately by notice from either Party if:

9.7.1 the other Party becomes bankrupt or is subject to a receiving or administration order, and/or goes into liquidation, and/or becomes insolvent (as defined in the Housing Grants, Construction and Regeneration Act 1996), and/or makes any arrangements with creditors

9.7.2 the other Party becomes unable to perform its obligations through death or incapacity.

9.8 On termination of performance of the Services and/or other obligations under the Contract, a copy of any drawings and documents produced pursuant to the Services and not previously provided by the Architect/Consultant to the Client shall be delivered to the Client by the Architect/Consultant, subject to the terms of the licence under clause 6.3 and payment of any outstanding fees and other amounts due plus the reasonable expenses of the Architect/Consultant.

10. Dispute Resolution

Mediation

10.1 Subject to clause 10.2, the Parties may attempt to settle the dispute, in the first instance, by mediation as specified in item K of the Contract Details.

Adjudication

10.2 Either Party may give notice at any time of its intention to refer a dispute or difference to an Adjudicator.

10.3 Referral of the dispute to an Adjudicator shall be made within 7 days of the issue of the notice.

10.4 If the Parties cannot reach agreement on a person to act as Adjudicator, either Party may apply for a nomination or appointment to be made by the Royal Institute of British Architects.

10.5 The adjudication rules shall be as stated in item K of the Contract Details.

10.6 The dispute may be referred by either Party to the final resolution process, as set out in item K of the Contract Details.

Arbitration

10.7 Where it is stated in item K of the Contract Details that arbitration applies as an alternative to litigation:

- **10.7.1** without prejudice to any right of adjudication, where in item K of the Contract Details an arbitration agreement is made and either Party requires a dispute or difference (except in connection with the enforcement of any decision of an Adjudicator) to be referred to arbitration then that Party shall serve on the other Party a notice of arbitration to that effect and the dispute or difference shall be referred to a person to be agreed between the Parties. If the Parties cannot reach agreement on a person to act as Arbitrator within 14 days of the date on which the notice is served, either Party may apply for a nomination or appointment to be made by the Royal Institute of British Architects

- **10.7.2** the Client or the Architect/Consultant may refer to litigation any claim for a financial remedy which does not exceed the financial limit provided by order made under section 91 of the Arbitration Act 1996

- **10.7.3** in such arbitration the Construction Industry Model Arbitration Rules (CIMAR) current at the date of the referral shall apply

- **10.7.4** the Arbitrator shall not have the power referred to in section 38(3) of the Arbitration Act 1996.

Litigation

10.8 Where it is stated in item K of the Contract Details that litigation applies, either Party may start court proceedings to settle a dispute.

11. Information Formats

11.1 Where produced using CAD, BIM or other proprietary software, drawings and documents shall be provided to the Client in PDF format only, unless an alternative format has been agreed and set out in item L of the Contract Details.

11.2 Without prejudice to the Architect/Consultant's obligations under the Contract, the Architect/Consultant does not warrant, expressly or impliedly, the integrity of any electronic data delivered in accordance with the provisions of item L of the Contract Details.

11.3 The Architect/Consultant shall have no liability to the Client in connection with any corruption or any unintended amendment, modification or alteration of the drawings and documents in digital format which occurs after they have been issued by the Architect/Consultant.

RIBA Concise Professional Services Contract 2020: Architectural Services

Schedule of Services

The specific Services that the Architect/Consultant will carry out at each stage of the Project are listed below. The Services will be undertaken in accordance with the stages defined in the RIBA Plan of Work.

This Schedule of Services **excludes** the role of **Principal Designer** as set out in the CDM Regulations 2015. The RIBA recommends that the default choice for the Principal Designer should be the Architect/Consultant, who should be appointed under a separate and distinct professional services contract (i.e. *RIBA Principal Designer Professional Services Contract*).

The Services being undertaken should be selected individually and ticked ☑ where an option APPLIES, provided that clause 3.1 and clause 3.2 of the Contract Conditions shall always apply.

Stage 0 – Strategic Definition

It is anticipated that services required as part of any Stage 0 – Strategic Definition activities will be commissioned on a time-based charge or as a separate professional services contract. However, any minor roles and services may be added if required.

- ☐ Provide feedback from previous projects
- ☐ Review relevant information from the Client to confirm the Client's strategic brief
- ☐ Other *(please specify)*

_____

_____

_____

Continue on a separate sheet if necessary.

Stage 1 – Preparation and Briefing

- ☐ Visit the site and carry out an initial appraisal
- ☐ On behalf of the Client, arrange the following surveys or other investigations that the Architect/Consultant identifies as reasonably required:

_____

_____

_____

© Royal Institute of British Architects 2020

- ☐ Contribute to the development of the Project Programme
- ☐ Establish the Construction Cost with the Client
- ☐ Assist the Client in developing the initial Project Brief
- ☐ Prepare and discuss feasibility studies for the Project
- ☐ Advise on the Other Client Appointments required to carry out the Project
- ☐ Provide a report on the feasibility of the Project for the Client's approval before progressing to the next stage
- ☐ Other *(please specify)*

_____

_____

_____

Continue on a separate sheet if necessary.

Stage 2 – Concept Design

- ☐ Prepare the concept design for discussion with the Client
- ☐ Coordinate the relevant information received from the Other Client Appointments with the Architect/Consultant's design
- ☐ Review and update the Project Programme
- ☐ Provide updated Construction Cost information to the Client
- ☐ Collate and agree with the Client changes to the initial Project Brief and issue the final Project Brief
- ☐ Provide architectural design information and identify the reasonably foreseeable residual health and safety risks to the Principal Designer
- ☐ Prepare a stage report on the concept design, final Project Brief and Construction Cost for the Client's approval before progressing to the next stage
- ☐ Other *(please specify)*

_____

_____

_____

Continue on a separate sheet if necessary.

Stage 3 – Spatial Coordination

- Prepare the design in sufficient detail to enable spatial coordination
- Coordinate the relevant information received from the Other Client Appointments with the Architect/Consultant's design
- Review and update the Project Programme
- Provide updated Construction Cost information to the Client
- Provide architectural design information and identify the reasonably foreseeable residual health and safety risks to the Principal Designer
- Prepare a stage report on the spatially coordinated design and the Construction Cost for the Client's approval before progressing to the next stage
- Prepare information to support a planning application and/or listed building consent application to the appropriate planning authority
- Submit a planning application and/or listed building consent application to the appropriate planning authority
- Other *(please specify)*

_____

_____

_____

Continue on a separate sheet if necessary.

Stage 4 – Technical Design

- Advise the Client of the planning conditions
- Prepare the technical design in sufficient detail to enable a tender or tenders to be obtained
- Coordinate the relevant information received from the Other Client Appointments with the Architect/Consultant's design
- Review and update the Project Programme
- Provide updated Construction Cost information to the Client
- Prepare the architectural specification/schedule of works* (**delete as appropriate*)
- Identify and agree the extent of the technical design work that is to be completed by the Contractor or the specialist subcontractors
- Prepare and submit the Building Regulations application
- Provide architectural design information and identify the reasonably foreseeable residual health and safety risks to the Principal Designer
- Advise the Client on potential contractors to be invited to tender for the construction works

- Collate the Other Client Appointments' tender information and issue the tender pack to the Client for its approval

- Invite, appraise and report on tenders

- Coordinate the design work prepared by the Contractor and the specialist subcontractors with the Architect/Consultant's design

- Advise the Client on the appropriate form of Building Contract, its conditions and the responsibilities of the Client, the Other Client Appointments and the Contractor

- Request that the Contractor provides evidence to the Client of any insurances required under the Building Contract

- Prepare the Building Contract and arrange for it to be signed/executed

- Coordinate and submit an application to the appropriate planning authority for clearance of pre-commencement planning conditions

- Provide the Contractor with the information reasonably required for construction

- Prepare a stage report on the technical design for the Client's approval before progressing to the next stage

- Other *(please specify)*

_____

_____

_____

Continue on a separate sheet if necessary.

Stage 5 – Manufacturing and Construction

- Provide architectural information to the Other Client Appointments, as reasonably required, to enable them to carry out their services

- Respond within a reasonable timeframe to site queries

- Provide the Principal Designer or the Principal Contractor with the architectural final construction issue information for inclusion in the Health and Safety File (under the CDM Regulations 2015)

- Provide the Client with the original copy of any notices, consents or approvals in connection with planning, building control and other relevant statutory approvals

- Maintain contract administration procedures, hierarchy of responsibility and lines of communication for the exchange of information between the Client, the Other Client Appointments and the Contractor in accordance with the Building Contract

- Organise, chair and record meetings, at the frequency stated in item F of the Contract Details, identify the activities to be undertaken and determine who is responsible for taking action and report on progress to the Client

- Carry out visual site inspections, as stated in item F of the Contract Details, to inspect the construction works with respect to general compliance with the Building Contract and Project Programme

- Certify interim payments in accordance with the terms of the Building Contract and advise on the final Construction Cost

- Review the progress of the construction works against the Project Programme

- Advise the Client regarding the effect that any variation or change proposed by the Client or Contractor will have on the Construction Cost and Project Programme

- Prepare and submit the application to discharge the construction-stage and the pre-occupancy planning conditions

- Issue instructions in accordance with the terms of the Building Contract

- Request manufacturers' maintenance instructions or leaflets from the Contractor and provide them to the Client

- Certify Practical Completion when this has been achieved

- Other *(please specify)*

_____

_____

_____

Continue on a separate sheet if necessary.

Stage 6 – Handover

- Carry out visual site inspections, as stated in item F of the Contract Details, and comment on the resolution of defects and issue site inspection reports to the Client

- Issue a schedule of defective works

- Liaise with the Client, the Other Client Appointments and the Contractor in relation to the making good of defects

- Inspect the remedial works following receipt of notice from the Contractor that the resolution of defective works is complete

- Certify when the defective works have been rectified

- Assist the Client and the Contractor to agree the final account and issue the final certificate

- Other *(please specify)*

_____

_____

_____

Continue on a separate sheet if necessary.

Stage 7 – Use

Services required as part of any ongoing (long-term) Stage 7 – Use activities are not listed. It is anticipated that such services will be commissioned as a separate professional services or operating contract.

Other Services

List any other services that the Architect/Consultant is going to undertake and state whether these are included in the Basic Fee (item F of the Contract Details), whether they will be carried out on a time-based charge, as per item G of the Contract Details, or whether they will be undertaken for a lump sum charge *(state the charge in the 'Other services' section of item F of the Contract Details)*.

_____

_____

_____

Additional Services

The following services are not included in the Contract but the Client can request that the Architect/Consultant undertakes these services, if the need arises, during the Project. These services are subject to additional fees, which are to be agreed between the Client and the Architect/Consultant.

Services may include, but are not limited to, the following:

- producing models and special drawings
- negotiating approvals with statutory authorities
- making submissions to and negotiating approvals with landlords, freeholders, etc.
- preparing a schedule of dilapidations
- services in connection with party wall negotiations
- negotiating a price with a contractor (in lieu of tendering)
- services in any dispute between the Client and another party
- services following damage by fire and other causes
- services following suspension or termination of any contract or agreement following the insolvency of any other party providing services to the Project
- services in connection with government and other grants
- specialist services in relation to historic buildings and conservation works.